Creatin Ed 11/3/05 DO $3.58

# START-UP
# RELIGION

# VISITING A CHURCH

Ruth Nason

# CHERRYTREE BOOKS

Distributed in the United States by
Cherrytree Books
1980 Lookout Drive
North Mankato, MN 56001

Library of Congress Cataloging-in-Publication Data
Nason, Ruth.
   Visiting a church / by Ruth Nason.
     p. cm. – (Start-up religion)
   Includes index.
   ISBN 1-84234-342-4
   1. Church–Juvenile literature. 2. Church buildings–
Juvenile literature.
   3. Methodist church buildings–Juvenile literature.
   I. Title. II. Series.

BV600.3.N37 2005
260–dc22
                                                2004064931

First Edition
9 8 7 6 5 4 3 2 1

First published in 2004 by
Evans Brothers Limited
2A Portman Mansions
Chiltern Street
London W1U 6NR
Copyright © Evans Brothers Limited 2004

Conceived and produced by

White-Thomson Publishing Ltd.

Consultants: Jean Mead, Senior Lecturer in Religious
Education, School of Education, University of
Hertfordshire; Dr. Anne Punter, Partnership Tutor,
School of Education, University of Hertfordshire.
Designer: Carole Binding

**Acknowledgments:**
Special thanks to the following for their help and
involvement in the preparation of this book: Rev. Peter
Barber, Rev. Sarah Lowe, Rev. John Fellows and all the
congregation at High Street Methodist Church,
Harpenden; the staff and children at High Beeches
Primary School.

Printed in China

**Picture Acknowledgments:**
John Barringer: page 15 bottom left; Chris Fairclough
Colour Library: pages 4 top left, 4 top right, 4 center,
4 bottom center; Michael Nason: pages 13 top right,
13 center, 13 bottom left, 15 top left.
All other photographs by Chris Fairclough.

# Contents

# Church Buildings

**Which of these buildings is a church? How can you tell?**

**There are many types of churches. The pictures in this book show the inside of this Methodist church.**

church          Methodist

**On a map, churches are marked with a cross.**
**How many churches are on this map?**

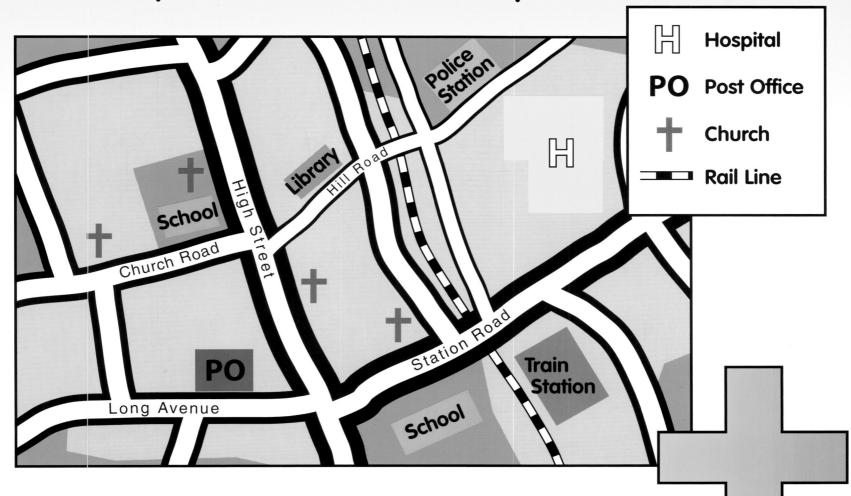

A cross is a symbol of Christianity. Can you think of places where you see a cross symbol like this? Look for crosses in the pictures in this book.

cross            symbol            Christianity

# Inside a Church

▶ On Sundays, many Christians **go to a service at church.**

A minister talks to the people. This church has three ministers.

The people at the service are called the congregation.

Christians    service    minister

Some churches have a **choir**.

▼ At the service, people think about **God**. They sing **hymns**, which tell God how they feel.

congregation   choir   God   hymns   **7**

# A Special Place

A church is a special place for Christians. They go there to worship God, to pray and to learn about Jesus.

They believe that Jesus is God's son, who taught people about God's love.

Can you see the picture of the baby Jesus in this stained-glass window?

special    worship    pray    Jesus

◄ The church is a quiet place to think and pray.

▼ What are these people doing to help make their church a special place?

believe        stained-glass        quiet        9

# A School Visit

When you visit a church with your school, it will probably be empty.

How do you think the people who worship there would like you to behave?

behave

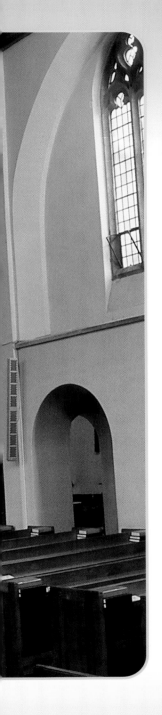

▲ **These visitors thought the church was:**

beautiful  big  quiet  pretty  peaceful

**They noticed details like these:**

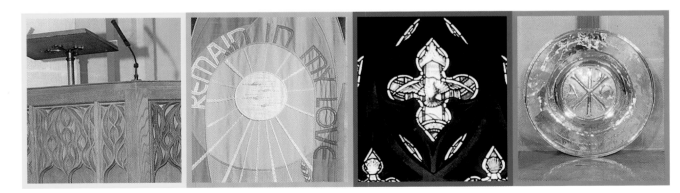

**Can you see these details in the big picture?**

details                    peaceful                    11

# Parts of a Church

The children saw that the church floor was in the shape of a cross.

Organ

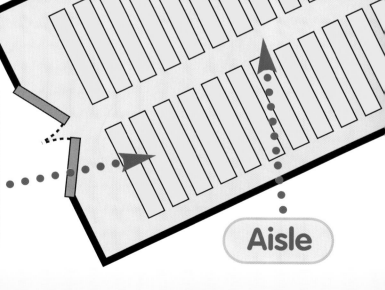

Aisle

▲ The minister asked if they could put names on parts of the church.

Pews

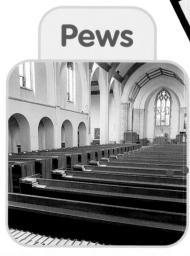

organ   pews   aisle   pulpit

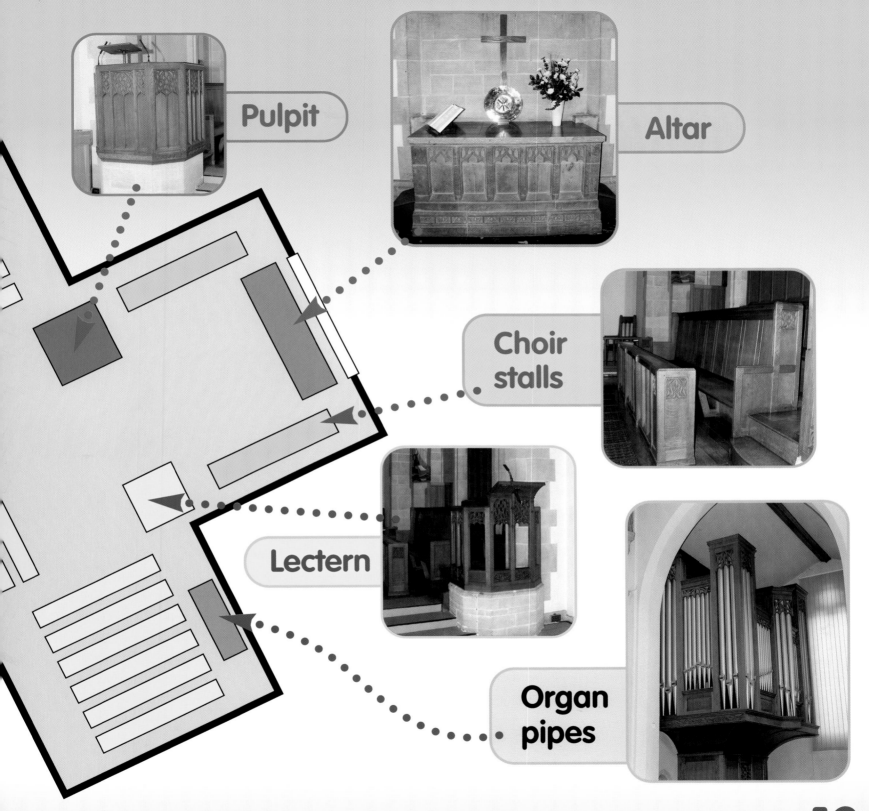

Pulpit

Altar

Choir
stalls

Lectern

Organ
pipes

**altar   choir stalls   lectern**

# Pulpit, Lectern, and Font

◀ In a service, the minister goes into the pulpit to talk to the people. This talk is called the **sermon**.

▶ Why do you think the pulpit is built higher than the church floor?

**sermon**          **Bible**

► **A lectern is a reading desk. In a service, someone stands at the lectern to read out part of the Bible.**•••••• **The Bible is the holy book with stories about God and Jesus.**

◄ **The font is used for a baptism. The minister splashes water on the baby's head.**

**holy book**          **font**          **baptism**

# Music in Church

Many people enjoy singing in church.

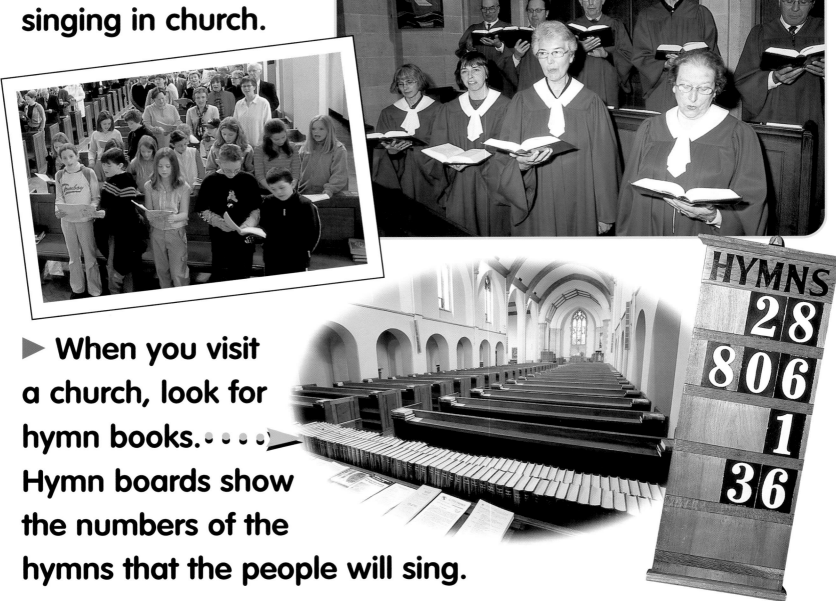

► When you visit a church, look for hymn books. • • • ►
Hymn boards show the numbers of the hymns that the people will sing.

HYMNS
28
806
1
36

▼ In many churches an organist plays the music for the hymns. He uses his hands on the organ keys and his feet on the pedals.

▶ The sound comes from the organ pipes.

organist    keys    pedals

# The Altar

► **The altar is at the front of the church.**

▼ **At communion services, the table is set with bread and wine.**

**Many Christians have services where they share bread and wine. Jesus told his followers to do this as a way of remembering him.**

communion services      share

◀ The minister breaks the bread.

▼ She shares the bread and wine with the congregation.

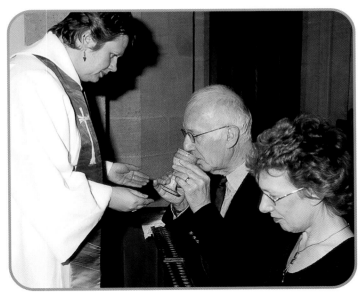

Above the altar is a cross. Jesus was killed on a cross, but Christians believe that he came alive again and now he lives with God, his father.

# Many Rooms

The church shown in this book has many rooms.
It is open every day, for people to visit.

◄ In the office, people help to plan the ministers' work.

► People come to talk to the ministers.

office          Sunday School

► There are rooms where the Sunday School meets on Sundays.

▲ There is a library and a café.

Can you see what happens in these rooms that is welcoming to visitors?

library    café    welcoming

# Further Information for

## New words introduced in the text:

| | | | | | |
|---|---|---|---|---|---|
| aisle | choir stalls | details | lectern | pedals | special |
| altar | Christianity | followers | library | pews | stained-glass |
| baptism | Christians | font | Methodist | pray | Sunday School |
| behave | church | God | minister | pulpit | symbol |
| believe | communion | holy book | office | quiet | welcoming |
| Bible | services | hymns | organ | sermon | worship |
| café | congregation | Jesus | organist | service | |
| choir | cross | keys | peaceful | share | |

## Suggested Activities

If possible, use this book in conjunction with a real visit to a local church. Consider using a "virtual visit", via a web site or CD rom, to supplement a visit, or if a real visit is not possible.

Videos and pictures of the church in use, and interviews with members, are useful supplements to visiting an empty building. This book can help prepare for such a visit and/or be used as follow-up. The church in the book is a Methodist church. Explore in what ways another church is the same or different. Try to avoid stereotypes by using resources showing a range of cultures if possible.

### PAGES 4-5

Take digital photographs of local buildings, including the school and churches. Let children identify them and sort them into sets. Link them to a local map for display.
Discuss same/different/similar.

Start a "cross collection" of pictures and label the places where they were seen (include jewelry and "crossed fingers").

### PAGES 6-7

Show a video clip of church worship.
Ask a member of a local church to come in to school and tell what they do there and how they feel about it.
Play the finger game: "Here's the church and here's the steeple, look inside and here are the people." Explain that the people are the church too, not just the building where they meet (cf. "a good school" can mean the people not the building).

### PAGES 8-9

Talk about the children's own "special places", private or shared, where they go to think.
Make a class list of all jobs needed to make a place special-interview the school janitor.

# Parents and Teachers

## PAGES 10-11

Talk about showing respect appropriately in different places (e.g. outdoor shoes off in gym, not jumping on grandma's sofa, not eating in stores). Prepare for suitable behavior in church, but don't make it intimidating.
If you visit a church, make time to be quiet and become aware of the atmosphere. Children's responses to it may vary.

## PAGES 12-13

Enlarge the plan of the church, or make one of the church you visit. Make cards of pictures and of names of church items- then play a "matching pairs" game and place them on the plan.

## PAGES 14-15

Ask someone from a local church to bring some items (e.g. Bible, hymn books, hassocks, cross, a crucifix) for children to draw and discuss so that they can recognize them on a visit. Find and read a Bible story the children know, and a hymn they may be familiar with (carols?).

## PAGES 16-17

Listen to tapes or videos of church music of various types ("gospel" songs or songs of praise as well as organ music). Play a math "find the hymn number" game with a "hymn board" if you can have access to a set of song-books.

## PAGES 18-19

Tell the story of Jesus' last supper (Note that it is not appropriate to role-play a communion).
Discuss how food can remind us of someone or some event, using children's own experiences. Discuss (and make?) what would be a good food symbol to remind them of a class event or known person.

## Recommended Resources

### BOOKS

Goody, Wendy, Kelly, Veronica, and Pruitt, Ginny. *A Peek into My Church*. Los Altos, CA: Whippersnapper, 1999.

### WEB SITES

The following sites provide a wide range of routes along which children can explore the significance of Christian beliefs and practices, and especially how these relate to worship in a church.

http://akidsheart.com

www.essex1.com/people/paul/biblea.html

www.missinglink.org/children.html

www.nowheat.com/grfx/family/religion.htm

## PAGES 20-21

If you go to a church, ask to see around various rooms. Look for clues about how the building is used by a living community, especially if it is a "historic" building. Avoid the impression that religion is something people used to do in the olden days.

# Index